Teen Can

Teen Devotional/Journal

written by Emmie R Werner

illustrated by Jack Foster

Halo
PUBLISHING
INTERNATIONAL

Dedicated to my fourteen grandkids–most
of them are TEENS, some pre, and some post!
I am so proud of you.

ISBN: 978-1-63765-186-5
LCCN: 2022902648

Halo Publishing International, LLC
www.halopublishing.com

Printed and bound in the United States of America

Dear Teen,

Welcome to a 21-day journey with God. He wants you to believe that with Him, all things are possible. Each day there is an I CAN scripture, short story, journal area, and writing prompt. This is your devotional/journal to write, draw, doodle, or paint your thoughts and prayers to God. It is between you and Jesus. I pray that this is the beginning of a great journey...believing...I CAN DO EVERYTHING THROUGH CHRIST WHO GIVES ME STRENGTH. Philippians 4:13 NLT

DAY 1

I CAN do all things through Christ who strengthens me.
Philippians 4:13 NKJV

Every day you or someone you know probably tells you what you can't do. Why is it so easy to put someone down rather than encourage them?

Let's look at the things YOU CAN do.

1. Make a list of all the things you can do.

2. Thank Jesus because He is the one who strengthens you to do these things.

3. Tell someone what you admire about them.

Journal

Write down some of your dreams. Take a look at your dreams, do your dreams honor God?

Remember:

I CAN do all things through Christ who strengthens me.
Philippians 4:13

Day 2

My Lord God in heaven has plenty of good and valuable things. Because you belong to Christ Jesus, God will give to you everything that you need. Philippians 4:19 Easy English Bible

This scripture says I belong to Jesus and He will give me everything I need.

Do you worry about what you are going to do with your life?

Do you worry about what to do when you graduate high school? College?

What does God's word say about your needs?

You can relax and trust God to supply ALL your needs.

Journal

What needs am I trusting God for?

Remember:

My Lord God in heaven has plenty of good and valuable things. Because you belong to Christ Jesus, God will give to you everything that you need. Philippians 4:19

Day 3

The Spirit God gave us does not make us afraid. His Spirit is a source of power and love and self-control. 2 Timothy 1:7 ERV

So many issues are facing me today.

Do I follow my peers? I want to fit in. Be accepted.

What do you want me to do God?

"I'm glad you asked," He replied. "I don't want you to be fearful. I want you to show love. Lead with my power."

That covers all my issues God.

"That's the idea my child."

Journal

In what areas do you feel fearful?

In what areas do you need to see God's power?

Ask Him!

Remember:

The Spirit God gave us does not make us afraid. His Spirit is a source of power and love and self-control. 2 Timothy 1:7

Day 4

...The only accurate way to understand ourselves is by what God is and by what He does for us, not by what we are and what we do for Him... Each of us finds our meaning and function as a part of His body. Romans 12:3-4 The Message

What are you going to do when you graduate?

Work? Where?

School/training? Where?

Maybe these questions cause you to feel anxious and uncertain of your God-given gifts. What a relief to hear God say – You find your meaning in life through Me. He has the road map. Ask Him!

Journal

List your top five gifts or talents.

How do you see these gifts being used for Christ?

Remember:

I find my life's meaning in God. Romans 12:3-4

Day 5

The Lord is my light and my salvation, I will fear no one. The Lord protects me from all danger. I will never be afraid. Psalm 27:1 Good News Bible

As you were growing up, who kept you safe? Was it a parent, grandparent, aunt, uncle, or older sibling? When you were with them, how did you feel?

Now think about what your heavenly Father says. Because of Him, you fear no one. He is your strength in every situation you could ever face. All of your concerns are His, you do not need to be afraid when you trust Him.

Journal

What situations cause you to be anxious or afraid? What steps do you need to take to trust God more?

Remember:

The Lord protects me – I will not be afraid. Psalm 27:1

Day 6

Children, you belong to God, and you have defeated these enemies. God's spirit is in you and is more powerful than the one who is in the world. I John 4:4 CEV

We all have a desire to belong, to the right club, the right crowd, the right family, and on and on. We think belonging to the right group makes us important, smart, attractive, or popular. However, what does God say? He says we belong to Him – our Father. Belonging to Him keeps us safe because He says so!

Journal

Where is a safe place for you? Why?

Remember:

I belong to God and God has defeated my enemies. I John 4:4

Day 7

But thanks be to God, who always leads us in victory through Christ. God uses us to spread His knowledge everywhere like a sweet-smelling perfume. 2 Corinthians 2:14 ERV

If I say, "I think I can, I think I can," what pops into your brain? Maybe someone read you "The Little Engine That Could" when you were small. You might think it is a kid story, but it is for any age. When the going gets tough, the tough unite with Jesus and we CAN!

P.S. If you haven't, read the children's book, "The Little Engine That Could."

Journal

Think of yourself being in God's parade. What would you be celebrating?

Day 8

But maybe you need to know how to be wise. Then ask God to help you. He is ready to give everyone what they need. And He never says it is wrong to ask. So God will help you to be wise. James 1:5 Easy English Bible 2018

Being a teen sometimes feels more like in-be-tween! So much is vying for your attention. Don't be afraid to ask for help, guidance, and wisdom. Your heavenly Father says it's never wrong to ask. Don't be afraid to pause, ask God for wisdom, and do what you hear Him tell you to do. He is always with you and wants you to walk in His wisdom.

Journal

Have you ever felt caught between what God wants for you and what your friends or social media wants for you? What can you do?

Remember:

Then ask God to help you. He is ready to give everyone what they need. James 1:5

Day 9

By deceit the king will win the support of those who have already abandoned their religion. But those who follow God will fight back. Daniel 11:32 GNT

How many times have you heard, "if you were my friend you would _____?" (fill in the blank) Deceit means to cheat or mislead. At the time, it may seem like an easy solution to a present problem, but Jesus says to deceive someone is to sin. His word says if you obey God you will be strong and resist the deceit of people who pretend to be your friend. It's only through Jesus you can be strong. Today say, "I can resist deceit with Jesus at my side."

Journal

Deceit, the very word, sounds scary. What types of deceit do you deal with in your life? How can you stand against it?

Remember:

But those who follow God will fight back! Daniel 11:32

Day 10

But then I choose to remember God, and this is my hope: The Lord's love never comes to an end. He never stops being kind to us. Every day we can trust Him to be kind again. We know that He will do what He has promised to do...He is the reason I can hope for good things. Lamentations 3:21-23,24 Easy English Bible 2018

What a promise that we can trust God! Every day we can trust Him. Trust between friends should be earned. Start being the friend that can be trusted and see what God does in your life. Good things come to those who put their hope and trust in the Lord.

Journal

Make a list of trustworthy traits. Who do you trust?

Remember:

But then I choose to remember God, and this is my hope: The Lord's love never comes to an end. He never stops being kind to us. Lamentations 3:21-23,24

Day 11

God cares for you so turn all your worries over to Him.
I Peter 5:7 CEV

Not everyone will know what struggles you face each day. It
might be a situation at home or school. Whatever is causing
worry in your life God has already taken care of it. Daily we
have to lay our worries at the foot of the cross and pick up
faith in our Heavenly Father. Faith that with Him we can daily
walk without worrying. He is right there walking beside you.

Journal

Put your worries in the can and turn them over to God.

Remember:

God cares for you so turn all your worries over to Him. I Peter 5:7

Day 12

The law says we are under a curse for not always obeying it. But Christ took away that curse. He changed places with us and put Himself under that curse...because of what Jesus Christ did, the blessing God promised to Abraham was given to all people. Christ died so that by believing in Him we could have the Holy Spirit that God promised. Galatians 3:13;14 ERV

Did you ever feel that no matter which way you go it is just not right, including obeying God? When you try to do right by God, but it seems that it never quite happens the way you want it to happen. When Jesus died on the cross He freed us from the curse of the law. He gave us the Holy Spirit to be with us, always guiding us. Have you asked Jesus in your heart? Have you asked the Holy Spirit to take control of your life, thoughts, and actions? He's waiting.

Journal

What do you struggle to let go of? How can you allow the Holy Spirit to help you with your struggle?

Remember:

Because of what Jesus Christ did, the blessing God promised to Abraham was given to ALL people. Christ died so that by believing in Him we could have the Holy Spirit that God promised. Galatians 3:13;14

Day 13

I am not saying this because I am in need, for I have learned to be content whatever the circumstances. Philippians 4:11 NIV

Looking around, we can always find a reason to be discontent. Instead, we can look around and count the reasons to be content. We think we need the latest, greatest shoes, phone, car, etc. Jesus sees to our needs and cares for us, but He wants our hearts to only need Him.

Journal

Make a list of all the things in your life you are grateful for. Is Jesus at the top of your list? 😊

Remember:

I have learned to be content whatever the circumstances. Philippians 4:11

Day 14

Christ has set us free to live a free life. So take your stand! Never again let anyone put a harness of slavery on you. Galatians 5:1 The Message

You might ask what is a harness and what could that mean to me? A synonym for the verb harness is control or direct. Today the right clothes, phone, achievements, friends, or social media might be harnesses to direct you away from what God wants for you. He said take your stand, and whenever He tells you to do something, you can know He is right there beside you–helping you stand strong.

Journal

What can you be free from? What would you take a stand for? Thank Him for His strength in standing with you so others might see Jesus.

Remember:

Christ has set us free to live a free life. Galatians 5:1

Day 15

If you belong to Christ Jesus, you won't be punished.
Romans 8:1 CEV

Have you ever thought or said, "I think God is punishing me for_____?" (fill in the blank) But that is not what the Bible says. If you belong to Him, He won't punish you. Now that doesn't mean we can do what we want, ask forgiveness, and just go on not changing. None of us are perfect, only Jesus, but with Christ in your heart, you can be assured He loves you and is for you every day.

Journal

How did you see Jesus in your life today? This week? This month? This year?

Remember:

IF you belong to Christ Jesus, you won't be punished. Romans 8:1

Day 16

Then instruct them in the practice of all I have commanded you. I'll be with you as you do this day after day after day, right up to the end of the age. Matthew 28:20 The Message

Have you ever stood up – looked around – and you are the only one standing? All alone, just you. We have all had those alone times when we feel no one is with us, understands us, or loves us. It's times like these that we must remember what Jesus says to us. He is with you always, day after day, 24/7. So, look around, do you see Him? Do you feel Him? He is always with you!

Journal

Can you think of a time when you felt all alone? What did you do? Now, what will you do if you are feeling alone?

Remember:

I'll be with you day after day – right up to the end of the age. Matthew 28:20

Day 17

...Become friends with God; He's already a friend with you. How? You ask. In Christ. God put the wrong on Him who never did anything wrong, so we could be put right with God. 2 Corinthians 5:20-21 The Message

Have you ever been blamed or punished for something you didn't do? Maybe it was a mistake, or maybe you were protecting a friend. If so, you know exactly how Jesus felt. He was blameless, sinless, and innocent, yet He went to the cross for you, for me, and for all mankind. How do you comprehend that? Your friend Jesus would do that for you. Believe it! He did it! You are so worth it!

Journal

Can you think of a time you were wrongly accused? Tell Jesus about it. Ask for His wisdom for future situations.

Remember:

God put the wrong on Him who never did anything wrong, so we could be put right with God. 2 Corinthians 5:20-21

Day 18

So because of all the things that God does for us, we can say this: If God is working on our behalf, nobody can really do anything against us. God did not even keep His own Son safe. Instead, He gave His Son to die on behalf of all of us. So certainly, God will continue to be kind to us. As well as His Son, He will give to us all things that we need. Romans 8:31-32 Easy English Bible 2018

Be aware of all God does for us every day. Even when we think He doesn't care, He is still working on our behalf. Little things that "just happen" to work out. People and relationships that "just happen" to cross our path. Blessings that "just happen" to come our way. Stop and think about it today. How did you see God working in your life today? (Be sure to thank Him.)

Journal

List the ways God has helped you today, big or little.

Remember:

If God is working on our behalf nobody can really do anything against us. Romans 8:31-32

Day 19

But in all these things we win a sweeping victory through the One who loved us. Romans 8:37 Common English Bible

Maybe you didn't get the grade you wanted or thought you deserved. Maybe you didn't get asked to go with 'the cool crowd' after the game. Or maybe you are putting yourself down. Think about this verse – a sweeping victory! Sweeping, big victory covers all relationships and thoughts. Remember this verse and how God swept away our worries and concerns by sending His Son. Never forget!

Journal

What are your worries and concerns? Ask God to sweep them away.

Remember:

You win a sweeping victory in all things. Romans 8:37

Day 20

When we meet together as God's people, He wants there to be peace among us. He does not want to bring trouble. I Corinthians 14:33 Easy English Bible

Buy this, use this, go here, stay there, and on and on. Before we know it we are sucked into a confusing mix of what the world says gives us happiness. But take a deep breath and look around. God has created peace when we pause to live in it. If you feel pulled in every direction or confused by the world, pause, and take a deep breath. Breathe in the peace that only Jesus offers.

Journal

What causes confusion in your life? What is the opposite of that, and how can you live there?

Day 21

I've told you all this so that trusting me, you will be unshakable and assured deeply at peace. In this godless world you will continue to experience difficulties. But take heart! I've conquered the world. John 16:33 The Message

When the Lord first asked me to write a TEEN CAN Devotional, I am ashamed to say I argued, told Him I'm not qualified, and I was not the one to write it. I should have answered yes, believing through Him and only through Him, I CAN do all things. As you continue your journey, be encouraged by God's word. Yes you will have some difficulties, but He is always with you, always beside you. He has conquered the world for you!

Journal

I CAN ...

Remember:

The Father is with me. I've told you all this so that trusting me, you will be unshakable and assured, deeply at peace. John 16:33

TEEN CAN ADDITIONAL ACTIVITIES

Day 1

Read the book "The Little Engine That Could."

Day 2

Today you learned God will give you everything you need – Think about giving something away.

Day 3

Today with God's power, do something totally out of your comfort zone.

Day 4

Volunteer at your church, school, or community.

Day 5

Is there someone in your life you could take under your wing to help them gain confidence?

Day 6

Is there someone, maybe not an enemy, but someone you need to take steps to make peace with?

Day 7

Read "The Little Engine That Could" again.

Day 8

What do you want to learn to do? Ask someone to teach you.

Day 9

Work out, run, walk, exercise. You are strong – physically and spiritually.

Day 10

Do an act of kindness for a stranger, neighbor, parent, or sibling.

Day 11

Write the scripture on a slip of paper; keep it in your pocket.

Day 12

Take someone's place today; give them a break.

Day 13

Gather clothing or food items to donate.

Day 14

Make a list of free activities. Choose one and invite a friend to join you.

Day 15

What groups/clubs do you belong to? Volunteer to do something extra.

Day 16

Is there something you have always wanted to do? Do It!

Day 17

Invite your friends to do something for no special reason, be a friend.

Day 18

Surprise someone with flowers, balloons, lunch, or coffee.

Day 19

Cheer for your favorite team. VICTORY!

Day 20

Take a walk, be still.

Day 21

Look at you – completed 21 days of TEEN CAN. Now encourage someone they CAN too!

Go to emmierwerner.com to see more TEEN CAN activities.

www.ingramcontent.com/pod-product-compliance
Lightning Source LLC
LaVergne TN
LVHW010310070426
835511LV00021B/3462